PERSPECTIVES

PERSPECTIVES

THROUGH THE LOOKING GLASS

AYLAH BIRKS

NEW DEGREE PRESS
COPYRIGHT © 2021 AYLAH BIRKS
All rights reserved.

PERSPECTIVES
Through the Looking Glass

ISBN 978-1-63730-660-4 *Paperback*
      978-1-63730-743-4 *Kindle Ebook*
      978-1-63730-934-6 *Ebook*

CONTENTS

CHAPTER 1 LOVE   9
    ATTACHING FEELING   10
    FLOWER PETALS IN THE WIND   12
    A GENTLE SMILE AND WARM TOUCH   4
    SELF WANTS   16
    LOVE INTERDEPENDENCY   18

CHAPTER 2 ATTACHMENTS   21
    YOU'RE ALWAYS ON MY MIND   22
    PEACE AT HOME   24
    LOVE AND PEACE INTERRUPTED   26

CHAPTER 3 SOCIETY   29
    SIGHT   30
    THE CROSSFIRE   32
    COLD TRUTH   34
    SOCIETY PT.1   35
    CANVASES   37
    SOCIETY PT.2   39
    LIFE BEFORE DEATH   41

CHAPTER 4 NATURE   **43**

    THE COUNTRYSIDE   45
    EVERYTHING WANTS TO BE SEEN   46
    FLOW AND FORM   49
    WATER WILD   51
    AIR   52

CHAPTER 5 SEASONS   **55**

    THE CORONATION   57
    HAPPY HOLIDAYS   60
    REFLECTION POINT   61
    LET IT GO   63
    SEASONS CHANGE   65
    GOLDEN LIGHT   66
    THINGS TO LOOK FORWARD TO   67
    SUMMER MORNING   69
    THE LAST DAYS   70
    THINGS REMEMBERED   72
    RETURN OF THE KING   73

CHAPTER 6 EMOTION   **75**

    INSPIRATION   76
    UNFILTERED EMOTIONS   77
    OUTFLOW   79
    FREE   80

CHAPTER 7 ANGER AND HAPPINESS   **83**

    FALLOUT   84
    TRIGGERED   85
    LIFTED   87
    FEELING SO UP   88
    SMILE   89
    SUPPORT   90

CHAPTER 8 SADNESS AND FEAR — **93**
    DESCRIPTION AND DEPICTION — 94
    A FEELING ARISING — 96
    INTRODUCTION TO FEAR — 97
    NO EXEMPTION — 98
    PARANOIA — 99

CHAPTER 9 WRITING TROUBLE AND UNCERTAINTY 101
    ORBIT — 102
    TRAIN TRACKS — 103
    MENTAL TRIP — 104

CHAPTER 10 BEING AFRICAN AMERICAN — **106**
    RAGE — 108
    TALES FROM THE SOUTH — 111
    THE QUESTION — 113
    AS I WAS — 114
    THE HORROR — 116
    THE DARK JUNGLE — 118

CHAPTER 11 BEING AFRICAN AMERICAN PT.2 — **121**
    BEING AFRICAN AMERICAN — 122
    THROUGH AND THROUGH — 123
    HAIR DEMANDS — 124
    AFRICAN AMERICAN WOMAN — 125
    THE IDEAL MAN — 126
    TO MY AFRICAN AMERICAN MEN — 129
    JOURNEY TO THE PAST — 132
    SOCIETAL SUNRISE — 133

ACKNOWLEDGEMENTS — **135**

LOVE

DEAR READER:
Love has the power to push through any sickness, disaster, or impossible feat. Having the power to hold true to the end allows it to begin again after that. As it circles around, it never allows you to just go through the motions when it's sincere.
Love is infinite and eternal, just as the trips are around the sun.
It reminds us of the good that is left in the world. Love has a way of wrapping us around its finger, having your nose wide open to hypnotizing smells dragging us throughout the hazy golden eyesight of flowery fields as time seems to slow down enough for one to enjoy everything in the moment.

ATTACHING FEELING

Love and attachment
Something I never expected to happen
It's that which sparkles
In its glory,

Gently holding me in their arms,
Blinding the danger
Allowing me to see the beauty and potential
In the fullness of my eyesight

Day to day
I am able to convey
Residing feelings
That I've housed for you

I find myself in a fit
Where I am nothing short of happiness
Having total support
Something of this world

You, my favorite version of comfort

"LOVE MAKES YOUR SOUL CRAWL OUT FROM ITS HIDING PLACE."

- ZORA NEALE HURSTON

Love led me out of the darkness that covered my life. I felt liberated, coming out of a jungle that haunted my night's sleep. I would find myself screaming in anguish and pain over the loneliness that consumed my day and crept over me during the night. The agony of feeling as if there was no one for me made living, more than life, coarse.
Finally, coming out of this jungle, I came into the lights of soft tones, causing my skin to glow.

FLOWER PETALS IN THE WIND

I felt lifted into the wind
Realizing we are petals
Blooming together on seasonal flowers
We don't wilt
But we are moved
Through the wind to various places
Reattaching ourselves,
And meeting again
Reincarnated in form and fashion
Just like freedom
Flying away like the prettiest bird

We conjoin and brush against
The moods of the day that switch
Our colors
On our canvases that were splashed
With the pollen that grew us so nicely
In the sunshine
Of the day in March

We grow together to grow apart
Independently interdependent
On each other,
Plucked and picked together
As chords on a guitar
Giving us room
To dance, to the tune of sweet songs

You,
Entertain me, chill me
Like the breeze
That blew us apart
As we remained together
Our flower petals never withered
Blowing along with the wind
To reach our destination
Together

WHAT IS LOVE
Personified is it so much, that it shows itself in its true form to us each day, while most of us fail to realize it.
We run away from it, scared because it is something new, and something never experienced. Speaking for itself through actions, it presents itself in the tiniest of ways, which have the grandest effect on our personalities and mentality.
Whether it shows itself in touch and bond, or looks and conversation, it takes a special instance for someone to grasp those feelings for someone else. Once it happens, it's as if rugged ground becomes clouds. The extremely harsh conditions become survivable, because you find joy in living and caring for not only yourself, but someone else as well.

A GENTLE SMILE AND WARM TOUCH

Love is
The kind look
That I'm able to find in your eyes

The mysterious adventure,
Not perfect, nor fine
That lasts one hundred lifetimes

Never falling, but walking
Into life, while unexpectedly
Melting the pain away
With trust and warmth
Suddenly is nice

The gentle smile,
With your warm embrace
I know that I can lean on you,
As you follow me, you become my shadow
Never leaving my side

It needs no voice
Because it is spoken for itself
Through actions, affection
Looks and sounds
But nothing describes it better
Than the gentle smile
And warm touch
Given from you to me

TO BE LOVED

The attachment that came along with love was the defining moment when I realized that this was where I needed to be. Within the hold of something and someone that I could finally lean and depend on, I felt secure. For the slightest touch and moment, I drifted away into a hazy subconscious where only space, time, and you reside. Driving towards the happiness, and that "pot of gold" at the end of the rainbow, everything was in sync.

SELF WANTS

I want to be loved
In a way
That welcomes me into the morning
After kissing my forehead
Sweetly at night

Knows what to say
Remembering that nine
Comes before ten
Something not disruptive
Or broken
That doesn't cut after a fight
Never causing a drop of blood
Something strong like stone

I want the type that builds me
Into a better me
That helps me towards my destiny
Consuming me, and grooming me
Into a better individual
That type of unconditional trust
Leading me, nothing here in vain

Something like a kid
In a candy store
I want something more
Something that can't be ignored
Something I can lead towards
Making me want to explore

The best love
Fitting like spandex
Or the right sized glove
Made me realize
That it comes from me first
And then someone else
Because no one does it better
Than you one the outside

LOVE INTERDEPENDENCY

The foundation
Supporting my love or you
Must first be
Strong enough to do
What I need it to do

The walls that I built
Around myself cannot crash
On any day
Because they support my sound
My image, and the space
Where my feelings lounge

I cannot love
If it doesn't first reside
Here for me
I cannot become interdependent on you
If I am not independent without you

CONCLUSION
As I found love, I decided to let it inspire the drive to create this chapter. The amounts of joy the I felt writing and reading this chapter was immense. Being able to discuss a broad topic with you honestly gives me much happiness. I hope that you got as much as I put into this chapter.

WISHING YOU ALL OF THE LOVE IN THIS LARGELY SMALL WORLD,

AYLAH.BIRKS.

ATTACHMENTS

DEAR READER:
As the sun beamed down on my face, expressions became beautiful, as you continued to look in my direction. As compliments and grins are exchanged in the following moments, we continue to enjoy the endless view of the ocean with hues of purple, pink, and light blue painting the sky in a beautiful tone. As time seems to slow down and speed by at the same time, laughs and sighs fill the air bringing us to build onto our connection that we've both longed for.

> "IN ALL THE WORLD, THERE IS NO LOVE FOR YOU LIKE MINE."
>
> - MAYA ANGELOU

YOU'RE ALWAYS ON MY MIND

From the very first time you smiled
I found it hard to concentrate for a while
The mystique of your presence
Your radiant glow in all essence

Your cocoa brown skin
Yes, indeed it shines in every light
So cool, but calm
You came to me
Seeing past my summer daze
And my sweaty palms

Giving me an unforgettable note
Filling it with the sweetest verse,
To my heart, I held it close
Watching you flash that unforgettable smile
You left me riding a wave that won't decline

IMAGES AND TICKER TAPE CELEBRATIONS

As the years pass by, and the road of relations winds and winds, there comes friction and noise. Too much noise and friction distract you from your purpose overall, but also does damage to the love that is being sent from one person to another. It causes true love to take a detour in which is gets damaged, battered, and arrives to you in an unwanted fashion. Unfamiliar sights and sounds are seen, as an uneasy and untrustworthy feeling arises in between the both of you. Questions and doubting concern arise just as the images and ticker tape celebrations that have been put up in front of those that watch seem to be ripping at every seam.

PEACE AT HOME

No peace at home,
Because I'm a mess at home

Putting up with everything you
chose to put me through,
for hours and hours,
of insults and nagging
I grow used to it and tired
my anger is ignited as my peace is disturbed.

Laying in my own bed,
sleeping but still tired,
and alive but not living.
The arguing and fighting,
leaves me breathless
because I love you so much
that I made myself lovesick.

You smell of her perfume,
Burberry No.1.
I hate the sight and view
of seeing you walk through my door.
I despise looking
into those eyes, deep brown.
No longer do I feel the sunshine,
but I feel thunder, lightning,
pain and a fresh frown made.

The regret of knowing
that I waisted me time and day,
Get out!
Because I only wanted one thing,
Couldn't have, trust, nor
Depend on it

Despite that I think so ethical
and you may find that my language
is rather colorful
I am not the justice
that is brought to you

I am so sick of you complaining,
with the kicking and the screaming.
You sound like a newborn child
that I've grown tired of babysitting.
I want the peace at home
that I was once promised

Alongside a love going unrecognizable, the person that you've committed to becomes that as well. It's as if they have morphed into a new person, that has had a change in attitude, walk, and demeanor. These are the things that make kind people turn, and only add to what a cold-hearted person has to offer. Digging a hole deeper around the situation causes everything that you have known and loved to fall to pieces.

LOVE AND PEACE INTERRUPTED

if loving you is wrong
let me know,
so I won't stay long
because your smile is so hypnotic
that I fall for its poison narcotic
nothing short of toxic

love an peace uninterrupted
turned violent orange,
crushed and unfit
if I have to cry each day
wearing a smile that's fake
let me go, and I'll never come back
because this love is off its track

a love and peace interrupted
led to merged lives to destruction

if you lie and leave each day
not caring how I feel, or what I say
buying gifts to hide the daily allegations
keep your receipts,

a love an peace uninterrupted
expired, and made my health disruptive

if we can't build each other for the better
be partners full of magic
like Penn and teller
save me the time and energy
because I've given you everything
that lies within me

a love and peace interrupted
pushed me away to leave on a high not adjusted

CONCLUSION
As attachments found their ways into my life, I was faced with the choice to either cut them off or keep them. Just as we always face these crossroads, not only in this category, but throughout life, our choice can take us of joyrides or nightmarish rides that chill us to our core.
I hope that you're able to reach and pass through your crossroads.

WISHING YOU ALL OF THE ATTACHMENT AND SEPARATION NEEDED IN THE WORLD,

AYLAH.BIRKS.

SOCIETY

DEAR READER:
What a beautiful mess of a society we find ourselves in. Tainted are the foundations upon which we live by. Morals have been abandoned for greed, as the daily news stations report the endless display of violence and committed crimes. In moments of hot desperation, rates grow higher beyond comprehension, and every day brings about a new struggle.
Welcome to Society.

SIGHT

The horror of everyday
Fazes me
Numbs me
Drowns me in my own tub
Of eventful actions
Who knew
Losing people I never knew
Made me miss them more
Watching George
Made me realize
They'll never come home
To twist that knob
But they'll twist their mouth
In agony over the wounds created

Caused me to change viewpoints
And perceptions
Angered me, and created resentment
Made me a feen for revenge
Shifted my vision
To the twisted vision
Of justice and foundational truths
The American reality
Uncapitalized and ceased the emphasis
On the American Dream
Because really,
A dream is nothing but
The false reality
That never seems to come true

"WHERE JUSTICE IS DENIED, WHERE POVERTY IS ENFORCED, WHERE IGNORANCE PREVAILS, AND WHERE ANY ONE CLASS IS MADE TO FEEL THAT SOCIETY IS AN ORGANIZED CONSPIRACY TO OPPRESS, ROB AND DEGRADE THEM, NEITHER PERSONS NOR PROPERTY WILL BE SAFE."

- FREDERICK DOUGLASS

THE CROSSFIRE

The price of freedom
Grows far away from free
Paying the price of life
As people are ripped
From flesh and bone
Inhumanity is praised
And pushed on a throne

Anger is the father of violence
Because here, the thunder comes
Following lightning
Striking anyone in deadly proportions
Driving them mad, and away from peace
While guns and drugs make them high
And out of their minds, they kill
Hindering their kind
Holding themselves and others hostage
The crossfire and aftermath
Can cause anyone
To deter off their own paths

The destruction carried out
by our own hands,
from our fathers and mothers
have stayed with us
haunted us, and followed us
our neighborhoods and communities
have done much to discourage
positivity in our children,
by exposing harsh reality and anger
towards their tender smile

and gentle hand
pushing them out into a world
that they know not of
nor understand
while also encouraging violent uprisings
throughout our globe.

Signed a life lease
that ripped us of the peace
that made up a piece of ourselves
that used to contain
sustain
and remain among us
to bank on the sun's trust
not afraid
rolled down the streets
more potholes and blight
than what could be counted
saw it to believe it
understood the assignment
before something had started to be done

poverty
foreclosure
debt
drugs
and money
all things suffered
a class gap
but way more than that
take notes and say cheese for the pictures
the war zone is upon us
full of violence and heavy hitters

COLD TRUTH

we venture not into the valley
of the source of the problems
the dark alley
we avoid to walk into
one can never complain
about the society they helped to create
either the problem was neglected,
or redirected
driving the act,
while being set up
they never let up
drowning in our own issue
trying to cover the breaks and mistakes
that marinate and carry weight
trying to move the money
which moved us

I talk about the cold truth, but honestly, I'm tired in a way that sleep can't fix. I wish to escape daily. Finding a way out of the supposed status quo is truly a want of indefinite proportions.

It seems as if freedom becomes more expensive, while shots are cheap, raising the blood pressure and adrenaline of anyone in or out of the system. Personal limits and nerves are pushed and snapped over periods of time due to the stress and fear of living in this crossfire.

SOCIETY PT.1

where in this day serves justice
public tabloids and life
all inhumane
no room for deep consolation
or solace
while the poor and unprotected peer out
of a broken and burned windowpane
at the violence leaving us traumatized
blood on the pavement
while shielding the sight from
our children's innocent eyes
as they run about, wild like cavemen

WHY SIT?
Enough pressure is not being applied. Issues that affect each member of the family goes on daily and too little is being done to stop it. However, someone must step up and take the mantle for our sake, our children's sake, and for the future generations. Someone must be willing to change their lives and be the domino.
We sit arguing on social media, while measures and discussions are left under a lit candle and table. Needing to be had and handled, we are incapable of listening to the realness and sense. As we continue to understand nothing, we go on to encourage cutthroat responses with no shame. The childish activities that stagnate our growth both anger and embarrass us all. Tangling ourselves with the mess of society, we gain a specialty in sitting idle and letting mass manipulation and gerrymandering control our mindsets.

As fear and mass hysteria convince us that we can only go so far, the media exploits and advertises it. And as art imitates life, our reflection is not only shown to ourselves, but to everyone.

Our stained canvas splattered with colors signifies the need for change, but shows the colorful blend of humiliation and disdain, bleeding with a heart of spiteful action and injustice.

CANVASES

Red, the blood splattered
in the city from the street murder
Dark Black Blue for the bruise of the night sky
falling over the city
burning constantly
full of rage and lies
with Gray undefined
full of blurred lines
in the judicial system
with a Boiling Orange, the runs the issues
with a hotline, White lines crack full
with a card cutting reality sniffing
in a straight line
Green for the contamination
of the mess we put our children through
Black shows us the darkness in us all
when we're driven
we wear White for the facade
we showcase on Sundays trying to be angels
and a Yellow caution light to come
alongside the Pink sentiment in our piece of mind
found in the quintessential kind
so it all adds up
to a canvas disarrayed
leaving you angry and dazed
full of colors changing
each day and week
creating the space where the narrative
remains the main topic
of how we speak and act

THE WAR ZONE

"WHAT'S DONE TO CHILDREN, THEY WILL DO TO SOCIETY".

- KARL A. MENNINGER

SOCIETY PT.2

bright embers from a fire
hot with passion
turn darker
than you could ever imagine

take the time to travel
to the unfortunate places
with potholes in the gravel
where the drugs are trunked
from the trees, roaches
smell loud like skunks

how can someone live here
where the sun doesn't shine
amidst all of it
where does peace exist?

"THE MOST DANGEROUS CREATION OF ANY SOCIETY IS THE MAN WHO HAS NOTHING TO LOSE.

- JAMES BALDWIN

Stepping out of the house, I couldn't help but feel my hair raise. Not knowing whether I will return at the end of the day is something that can rock anyone, if they focus on it too much. The immense pressure that I'm under to make it home, goes unnoticed. It's as if I don't only want to have life, but live, before my alarm goes off.

Seeing so much violence these days cuts that chance by a major percentage. It causes me to think twice about life itself, and personal relationships. Each day, it seems as if some go before their lives begin to start.

I feel propelled towards a horizon that pushes me to want to live a life with no regrets or stress.

LIFE BEFORE DEATH

I'd like to have a life before death
not to be stolen like a criminal theft
because before I could ever start to live
I would have already left
been late on life, the prize
with an early demise
due to stereotypes made by some people
that set low heights knowing
that they've always wanted me down
whether emotionally,
or six feet in the ground

never have I wanted that chance
to leave early
without finishing that last dance or
check out this earthly residence
with urgency before being able
to see fun commence
leaving the memories behind
wishing
that fate was more kind
to my young soul
allowing me to mature and grow old

seeing another trip around the sun
seems impossible
because
the time has runover the clock,
and out of the earth
I tell my mother,

I miss her,
because I loved her first.
I plant a seed and let it grow
in age and beauty
something that I would never show
because I had no life before death
and nothing else left.

CONCLUSION

My greatest wish for youth worldwide, and for you reading this book is to reach you stride, goals, and everything that follows. I wish for you to be able to see yourself successful through whatever measure that may be. Don't fall by the wayside of society. I want you to live your life to the fullest, and fill it with excitement and happiness, in which you can only do. Remember, glasses don't fill themselves. Don't the crossfire grapple you and pull you down to your lowest points. I hope that you find a way out of any tough situation that you land yourself entangled in through this society. Although this world isn't easy, I think it's best that we begin to unite as sisters and brothers to create the change and society that we would like to see.

WISHING YOU ALL OF THE HOPE FOR SOCIETY IN THE WORLD,

AYLAH.BIRKS.

NATURE

DEAR READER:

Nature opens the soul, frees the mind, and gives us a feeling that lasts a lifetime. Think of the grass that may grow through a crack, or new islands that form from rock and ash.

I know that diamonds form under pressure, and that rainbows emerge after a thunderstorm's pleasure.

As birds fly overhead during sorrowful times, I see the hope that shows and the healing that begins, as if it's written for us in the sky.

What is it about the outside that is so tranquil and easygoing? It's as if everything bends with the winds and gives reverence to that of the highest. Think of how everything begins to brighten up as soon as the sun takes its daily stride. The birds begin their conversations, while the roosters crow and serve as nature's alarm.

Not to mention how trees give endless rounds of applause, with help from the winds that gust a melodious bow. Everything commences in order to give a grand introduction into a day that is freshly created and will never be seen again.

EARTH

HEAVEN IS UNDER OUR FEET AS WELL AS OVER OUR HEADS

- HENRY DAVID THOREAU

We trod and trudge, but the Earth won't budge. She is mighty and firm, although her body twists and turns. Landmarks are carved within her ground, as the moon orbits her round and round. Feet gracing the grass grown, while new seeds are sown.

Hills and mountainous landmarks are surrounded by national parks. We must remember that this is ours to inherit, and that it's a family artifact meant for us to cherish.

THE COUNTRYSIDE

I rode upon a road
Dusty and uneasy
Through the beauty of the countryside
Sweet sounds that coincide
With the calmness, beauty, and pride
That lies in my heart, and forever resides
Here in the crook of the countryside

The trees, full of the richest green
The swaying flowers
Waltzing slow, but purposefully, it would seem
While the tall grass bends with the wind
And the ground bears the fruits within
Sprouting upward, with field of wheat gold
Every day brings a new persona, nothing old

White clouds in a sky filled with blue
Along with the feeling of the slight breeze that blew
Right through my hair and back up to the sky,
The serenity that came upon me
Causing me to forget my identity
Wrapping me in the beauty of nature's hand inside
Here in the crook of the countryside

EVERYTHING WANTS TO BE SEEN

Ever notice this little thing
I call it the attention zing
How nature on Earth wants to be recognized
Looked upon, admired and prized
Everything does something to be seen
Understand what I mean?

Notice how trees do everything but walk for attention
It's the little things that should be mentioned
With their leaves blowing, exhaling,
and changing from old to new
There branches of arms rocking
to the rhythm of the wind that blew

Flowers do the same
Their full, stylish structure is to blame
Blooming beautifully
Each spring for you to see
Sprouting about in your yard
While their scent grabs you, holds you
And makes ignoring hard

The sky is in this tale too
Whether it's stained red or sporting bright blue
Some days, throwing tantrums everywhere
Throwing about baggage without a care
It screams and booms
Making sounds that shake pictures in a room
And how could you forget the sight
Of floating elephants that appear white

Turning gray when they begin to dance
Rapidly spinning, and changing at every chance
It wants to be heard and seen
With no feelings in between

At last the animals that live and grow up
Living each day just to show us
Think of the birds making noise
Doing nature's announcements
While the ants construct new hilly monuments
Bees dance
and leave their marks
on the world's face
While bears mark their territory,
roaming around in their space

Everything just wants to be noticed
Always seen and not missed
Given attention, and not neglected
Where they all have a place in this world,
Being respected

WATER

> "THEY BOTH LISTENED SILENTLY TO THE WATER, WHICH TO THEM WAS NOT JUST WATER, BUT THE VOICE OF LIFE, THE VOICE OF BEING, THE VOICE OF PERPETUAL BECOMING."
>
> - HERMANN HESSE

FLOW AND FORM

Be calm
like the freshwater stream
that flows through the woods year-round,

Allow easiness and peace of mind
with whatever you do,
or wherever you go.
Wherever you choose to pass through,
Let life surround you.
The appreciation level of respect is personal.

Provide the stability and sustenance
for those that need it.
Moving through the world in your own way

You might not have the strongest flow.
There may be some twists and turns, because
At times, there may be blocks,

but a flow cannot be stopped
Solutions and detours will be made
in order to maintain the flow and form

"WHILE WATER CAN PRESENT ITSELF IN DIFFERENT WAYS, FALLING FREELY OR WILD, IT IS THE LIFE AND SPIRIT THAT EMBODIES THIS EARTH"

- AYLAH BIRKS

THE STORM

Water can be just as dangerous as it is welcoming. The anger and fury that can be found within its heart, can rage on for hours upon days, with its effect lasting long. Washing away things old, needed, and cherished. It is deep, dark, and dangerous. Nothing should be unexpected as well as expected. The look of the sea full of uncertainty speaks for itself, as unimaginable events are witnessed before your very eyes.

WATER WILD

Razor sharp and ice cold
Wild and unhinged,
crashing on shore
An ocean,
black as coal
Rocking rapidly,
it never folds

AIR

Air brings life into this world. It gives us the push or pull to resume or start new chapters in life. It pushes us in our direction forward to new horizons, or pushing us backwards, repelling us and challenging us.

Air knows where to be most noticeable, and where to be unnoticeable. If it is bored enough, you might hear it talk to you, through its wind. Wind brings life to air, just as air brings life to the Earth. Wind is character, mood, sound, and motion on this Earth. Whether it's a slight whisper, or a loud howl, the air, and wind itself will speak and make its presence felt.

AIR

As time flew
The birds did too, through the air
Pure and continued
To fill the void of life left loose
On one of those calm days, without the wind

I was able to breathe
The area clean, with air
Of crisp quality filtered by trees
Walking on cloud nine, feeling mighty and pleased

While the wind brought rhythm and dance
I did well to take a chance
To listen and have a glance

Freedom called
Seen through the seasons each
And I then heard the voice
Of the wind and all
Where the sweet songs of life and happiness
Stood firm and tall

Think of the breeze that blew through your hair. As it lifted, you felt lifted along with it, as if you were walking on air itself straight into clouds. While giving your hair to the wind, you softly smile. Letting go of the stress that life brings gives different feelings of joy and freedom. Feelings of full volume, independence, and confidence were some of the sweet gifts that the element of air had dropped into the soul.

The windy tune made the day give way to the breeze that carried everything off to tomorrow's land. It propelled me forward, never letting me go. I felt free as a bird here, like those that soar from cages unseen. Feeling like the birds that accelerates trough the skies, I sped through time from summer to winter. The wind gave rhythm to the leaves gracing ground, as they traveled

CONCLUSION PT.6

DEAR READER,

This chapter is rich with peace, nostalgia, and depth. As I bring this chapter to a close, the beauty that is captured in these stories and poems compares not to what is seen within the naked and inside eye. Beauty is in the eye of the beholder, and frankly, I've found that a fragment of that beauty residing here in this chapter.

While trying to cover the major elements within this planet, understand that it is all done out of love and respect. These two things go hand in hand throughout the course of this chapter, as well as this journey. May the beauty and joy of this course carry you to reach new heights throughout this literal journey.

WISHING YOU ALL OF THE NATURAL INTERACTIONS IN THE WORLD,

AYLAH.BIRKS.

SEASONS

DEAR READER:

We find ourselves continuing the timeline of nature throughout the seasons of the year. Throughout each of them presents beauty in unique aspects, tones, and description.

WINTER

> "I PRAY THIS WINTER BE GENTLE AND KIND - A SEASON OF REST FROM THE WHEEL OF THE MIND."
>
> - JOHN GEDDES

I woke up with a February gaze, as I thought of the meals carrying me throughout December, and the scares from October pumpkin grins. As I walked the thin line between time and temperature with shorts and sweaters, I heard the hollow tree round. Its foreboding arrogance in its presence whistled towards winter.

I felt the tick of the clock, knowing that time is moving on in the air. However, it stayed in place to allow everything to acquire movement and flow. Kicking it back to demo tapes and mega mixing tapes, time rolled from Spring Break to Winter Break.

As I took it all in, I hummed and heard the late winter song walking down the road.

THE CORONATION

As the King and Relaxation stepped down
It left its title once more, and passed on the crown
For all things must come and go
The new queen is here to put on a show

And her parade hit on the start of a November night
Her horns blew loudly, but still no sight
No change in scenery
Of her majesty the queen to be

Morning came painted with ice and white
She silently approached us in a fashion throughout the night
As she triumphed trees bowed
As she waltzed leaves applauded loud

Her crowning happened on the solstice
Beauty full with much cold bliss
As fall left with one last bang
He left not without crowning her, while her horns rang

When she came around,
everything came to a screeching halt
and bowed down to her.

Leaves left on branches
gave her a round of applause
after her winds came through
during her daily parade
through valleys and vast lands.

While moving on,
she did her deed
to leave
an abundance of food
on below each shade,
behind each crook,
and near each cranny.

Looking in awe,
several bands of animals
scrambled around. Watching intently
as squirrels eat, and store,
and birds circle around,
reach, and soar away,
while the others sit and watch,
only to save their harvest
for a later time and date.

The ice queen of cool has made her triumphant return to Earth. As she begins to close out the season, she strips everything bare. All things take on a raw shape and form, bearing everything nature has given and put it though during the year. Winter shows things up in its true form. Her presence is felt far and wide, as we bundle up in itchy sweaters and scarfs in a warm house for a lazy day.

THE HOLIDAZE AND HOLIDAYS
As the world turns about to another winter season ending trip around the sun, we find ourselves located in the part of the year where holidays make headlines. We often hear about the thanks for giving, wishes for snow, and preparations for the new and upcoming year.

The preparation for Christmas and Thanksgiving comes with anticipation. This thought of seeing relatives from the present, remembering those of the past, and anticipating those to come all brings smile to faces of many. Not to mention, the long tables full of food, stories, laughter, and impending family drama, are all things expected and unexpected during the blessed holidays. It's those moments there that we all look forward to.

HAPPY HOLIDAYS

Coming from the distance
With mileage heavy on my pocket
I find myself as the apprentice
Prepping for dinner and building a rocket

Wrapping the trees and stringing the berries
Climbing the stairs with boxes and bins
Stepping into the kitchen with all that I carry
With embraces met with wide grins

These are the moments and times
Made by the people you love
Imperfectly perfect every try
While the snow falls above

I sat down to realize the real truths
And grab some food while I was at it
About the stories and the lessons told at my youth
The holidays were here, time to relax lavish

REFLECTION POINT

The daze
one like no other.
While reflecting
over a year of joy and laughter,
there are some pieces
unhappiness,
guilt,
loss,
and sadness
that nudge their way
into your reflection.

It's not just you,
it's all of us.

It's been a tough year.
Losing the people, you love
aren't always the best ways
to end off a year,
nor is seeing hostility and anger
dealing with the guilt
and hurt of a lover's past
or friendship gone seems
to take a huge portion of the cake.

I personally think that
the worst type of separation
happens during the holidays.
For some reason, they seem
to heighten
suspense,
drama,
and hatred coursing through actions.

LET IT GO

Release
Find peace
Hold it not in your heart
Reflect
Shed tears
But never neglect
Yourself
How you feel
Because stress really does kill
Your vibe, your life
Changes plans
And makes you switch hands
Kiss away your fears
Tell grief goodbye
And walk on the lighter side
Let not your heart be troubled
With things of the past
Because moments never seem to last
Let it go
And start fresh
Because you deserve to be your best.

CONCLUSION
DEAR READER:

As we find ourselves wrapping up the year with another Winter, and transitioning into Spring, I wish for you the warmest of sweaters and socks to get you through the cold days and freezing nights.

Happy holidays and best wishes to you if you find yourself stumbling over this little section during the festive and

frosty side of the year. Take some time to admire things as they are and look in your heart to spread that warmth whenever you feel cold.

WISHING ALL OF THE WARMTH AND HUGS OF LOVE IN THE WORLD,

AYLAH.BIRKS.

SPRING

As late winter rolled away, highly common and uncommon things occurred in spring. Indeed, the season in between those with two different reasons brings much to the table in surprise and fun, but also in suspense and need. Personally, the occasional late snow that wasn't given in January returned to grace us with a post card from winter and fall.

SEASONS CHANGE

Now it was a new day and age
I jumped onto the winds to ride a wave
Something felt warm, while I felt cool
Honeybees flew under me, the buzz gave me fuel
I left my hair to the breeze
The peace left me on ease
Blossoms and budding on treetops and hills
Butterflies landed on my fingertips,
anointing me with a seal
I felt the love of a welcome,
saying goodbye, the cold
Seasons change,
I felt new, young, and bold

GOLDEN LIGHT

The yellow pollen aggravating
my nose and keeping it stuffed
to its bunches.
I felt heavy with a 20-pound head,
larger than spring's presence itself.
Hobbling
from side to side,
I felt dizzy,
as well as the wind
from bees and bugs set me free.
Bouncing from a low high
I swiped and reached
for the butterfly that flew away
I fell to the ground
in a fit of aggravation and laughter,
seeing that spring is really the bee's knees.

THINGS TO LOOK FORWARD TO

Rainy days
Made me drowsy beyond comparison
Endless weekends in my teenage times
Smelling peaches to pick
And running through fields golden
Bless those springtime feels
That made me smile all day
Cheeks red and rosy
Doleful and hazy
1080p lens with a blur on life
Not sure on what happens next
Finding my next chance on the next
Dandelion to dance

CONCLUSION

DEAR READER:
as spring wraps up, I begin to take in the last blooming of the season, and the comfortable weather. Looking back on the windows of rainy days, and nights of unlimited stuffing brought me to a slight chuckle, as I reminisced on other things that ran through my mind. I hope you remembered to smell your flowers sometimes, and blow dandelions for peace and comfort.

WISHING YOU ALL OF THE WARM RAYS AND RAINY DAYS OF GROWTH IN THE WORLD

AYLAH.BIRKS.

SUMMER

> "AND IT WAS THEN THAT I REALIZED EVERYTHING THAT I EVER WANTED OUT OF LIFE WAS HERE. HAPPINESS, FONDNESS, AND SUNSHINE WERE THE REMEDIES THAT HEALED ME FROM A LONG YEAR OF SCHOOLING."
>
> – AYLAH.BIRKS

I remembered the things that spring brought close and near. As the heat started to increase, so did the fun and the iconic kodak pictures.

I said goodbye to my morning sweaters and my allergy routines for sunglasses and sunscreen, with beaches in mind, I fell back into the times and the arms of an upcoming summer on the horizon.

SUMMER MORNING

ghetto birds' tweet
at the crack of dawn,
outside is stuffy or dry,
the ice cream truck rolls
through the neighborhood,
and the heat becomes high,
smiling to myself,
remembering that you have no school,
with no papers; assignments; or drama.
Instead, you have only one responsibility,
have fun.
Days in the shade of grand tree or running through a field of flowers with the wind propelling you forward to your destination.
The very nature of summer is that of an unforgettable vibe. Things seem to fall into perfect place, while tranquility and live wire energy combine to give you the time of your life.

THE LAST DAYS

Candles burning for wisdom and peace
Entertainment is my rainstorm to say the least
Outros and interludes
In and out of the day that protrudes
We are in the last days
Of summertime shade

Sending you cards to wish you well
Surfing on sun waves so clouds could tell
Riding on moonlight with golden skin
Coming home late, overflowing within
Weak in knees from the weight of love
While my head flies into altitude above

Rockets to endless locations
Down highways of great expectations
The orange sun is slowly falling
As the day becomes largely quiet and stalling
Feeling the things that should be felt
These are the last days in deck being dealt

CONCLUSION

ALTHOUGH THE CHILL TEMPERATURES AND SLOW PACE OF IT MAY NOT CLEARLY RESEMBLE THE BUSTLE OF SUMMER. I HOPE THAT THIS PIECE HAS GIVEN YOU AN ESSENCE OF SUMMER THAT YOU NEVER FORGET. REMEMBER, AS SEASONS BRING ABOUT CHANGE, SO DO THE PEOPLE SURROUNDING YOU, FOR BETTER AND WORSE.

MAY THE BEUATY AND HEAT OF THE SUMMER RESIDE IN YOUR SOUL FOREVER.

WISHING YOU ALL OF THE OCEAN BREEZES IN THE WORLD,

AYLAH.BIRKS.

FALL

THINGS REMEMBERED

Remember the laughs here
The life and love kept
As the simplicity and calmness took over fears
While the slight chill crept
Up the spine and through the bones
But quickly booted out
By family and reconciling shouts

Starry night
A full moon looking bright
Illumination to the eyes and life of fall
Nature gave it's all
And the product is ours to reap
In bunches and bundles, that form heaps

A dinner table full with food
Endless amounts of hugs set the mood
Of thanksgiving and gladness
No room for the drama that brags mess
But focusing on the good the life has to bring
Not worrying about the issues from last spring
But focusing on the things remembered
Giving us joy from September to November.

RETURN OF THE KING

Relaxation and chill
Fall at its finest
The love experienced at your own will
Bring you joy in the form of the shiniest

Although things become slow and smooth
Some things just don't change
Such as unforgettable times had in your shoes
And laughter louder than you can explain

Nature settles on its throne
For a period of rest and preparation
To nurture and nestle,
My how this time has flown
Through January cold and October creations
The year is almost at its close
But still keeping interest and life on its toes

Dark colors that compliment and speak
Describing how you feel
Bringing out you inner beauty throughout your week
The glow, undeniable,
Nothing here is surreal

Peace and Zen are the moods
Because the king of relaxation and chill has come
And Fall is back in its groove

CONCLUSION

I personally see fall as the time to rejuvenate and restore. It's as if life itself hits not only the pause but the rewind and remind button. It reminds you of the times when you must take time out to find your inner self, and relish in those moments. On top of that, I think it reminds you to be grateful for the predicaments and blessings that are bestowed upon you. Even though the "King of Relaxation and Chill" does everything to warm you up to the season and what it may bring, self-development and personal reflection allow you to settle and focus on the things that matter the most.

It's nothing like a season that allows you to recap on your year and slow down for a while. As the year winds down, you take a moment to sit back and relax as the leaves blow through, while the winds rock the trees to a day's rest. The imagery and moments here are more than special. They are things remembered for years to come.

WISHING YOU ALL OF THE FUN AND MEMORIES IN THE WORLD,

AYLAH.BIRKS.

EMOTION

DEAR READER:

Emotion is something that runs further and deeper that human understanding itself. It constantly changes, just like life. It is never stagnant. Emotions allow us to shape our lives the way we see fit, and it propels us towards new horizons.

I am truly alive, and in touch with who I want to be. It's nothing like being able to really express how you feel. Not feeling bound by the branches or ties, I feel the freedom that many people long for each day.

INSPIRATION

The greatest reactions
Run live with presence
Reactions that created our lives
Oddly beautiful in their own right

Just as a journey is one in its own
Seen with the nakedness of the eye
Touched
Imprinted
Felt
An emotional state

They play out
Contained octane and color
Polar opposites
Successful eruptions
Smiles and balance
The yin and yang
Found within Happiness and Anger

UNFILTERED EMOTIONS

Raw, uncut, and uncensored commotion
Seeping out like honey from the comb
The unfiltered emotions
Which tore my heart, and left me alone

Days that are perfectly good,
Highly uncommon
Others are like a sea of stormy waters
Not even summoned
Happiness, like on a summer's eve.
Sadness, like cold tears, heartbreak,
Or a time to grieve.

Feelings unfiltered,
That flow wild and free, like the river.
Nervousness and sweat,
That pour, like rain out of a cloud.
Confident, and robust,
Indeed, just like a citrus tang, a flavor that's loud

There is no filter.
Everything is pure, and in its rawest form.
Like a newborn child,
Innocence to adulthood,.
A budding life, or something torn.

Not sure how to feel,
Strong and tough,
Like the orange peel.
Or soft and smooth,

Like a marshmallow with puff.
Maybe loud with screams and cries
Tell me would you rather yell, or silently sigh?

Do you take the time to breathe
Or do you not choose to relieve
Yourself when under pressure
Whether on the inside dealing with the outside weather
For worse or better

Raw, uncut, and uncensored commotion
Seeping out like honey from the comb
The unfiltered emotions
Which tore my heart,
And left me alone.

OUTFLOW

The madness that ensues
From a faucet overwhelmed with outflow
Full of emotion, rich with content to show
Presents itself outstandingly in a loud hue

Knocking you into subconsciousness
Where you are usually unaware
Of the absence
In the time and presence
That you share
With the feelings falling
In numbers countless
Every and anything here is far from emotionless.

FREE

What happens when emotions becomes unfiltered
and free?
Does it roam quietly,
Or does it leap energetically,
Like a frog to a tree?
Do all of your feelings come to life?
Or is the tension between them so thick,
That you cut it with a knife?

Tell me, what do you feel?
How do you react?
Are you stunned?
Does it seem unreal?
The emotions
They are wild, but not compact
And what we feel, we cannot take back

The rush of adrenaline,
Does it course through your veins?
Running hot like lighting within
On a summer's eve, accompanied by rain
Or is the feeling tranquilized,
Sneaking upon you like the moon on a cloudy night?

Do you blossom like a lily in a valley
With a new look, and personality?
Do you find a way to contain it, and channel the energy
Censoring it to a degree?

CONCLUSION

DEAR READER:

There is no filter here. No love to express like mine itself is obvious here. I find myself stumbling n actions and chances to express my words to convey. Filling my face with the feelings unspoken are somewhat exciting me at the thought of releasing. My expression is my own, as I fill my empty cups with the fuel powering the need to know. I choose to drink from freedom and expression unfiltered.

WISHING YOU ALL OF THE EMOTIONAL FREEDOM IN THE WORLD,

AYLAH.BIRKS.

ANGER AND HAPPINESS

DEAR READER:
Anger, to me it feels as ferocious as a category five storm surge, or like a lion when he hunts prey. The emotion can last year long or be extinguished in a quick manner.
Possibly, you could think of happiness where everything is as good as gold. Things seem to take on this new glow of radiance, which blocks out the darkness that may haunt you in the back of your mind.
It can make you scream, cry, laugh, and feel a high that you may never want to come down from. When you're happy, you feel free, and once you're free, you'll fly, and once you fly, the sky is a limit.

FALLOUT

Do you really know how I feel
Understand that my expressions are a diversion
Unseeing what is there, and what is real
An unreadable anger,
Something deemed unimaginable for me to act in
Because I'm labeled kind, anger can't be a caption
Silent is the distant storm
Arising is the captivating form
Of something hot that doesn't burn
And something cold causing you to turn
Create a fallout, shock everyone
Through blunt honesty, and frustration
A swift kick to the side
While this was something unexpected
It unfolded, and released itself hectic.

BOILING OVER

It pecks at you, forms a crust over you, and finally takes control. But tell me, what happens after the anger is gone, and you come back to yourself? What happens when your subconscious level is out of fuel, and you go back to relying on your consciousness? It's like returning home to see the damage after a natural disaster has struck your area. You see that there is damage done, with some being able to be fixed, while hope is lost for others. Things have been said that could have been labeled as "way too far", but the damage is already done. Before thinking about what to say, things were blurted out with the quickness. It's like shots being fired, and the battle for who has the quickest gun starts. In this case the trigger is hidden within the mind and pulled by words pouring out of the mouth.

TRIGGERED

As hurt
and dehumanizing comments resurface
No one stops
until it is all
said and done.
A cloud of silence reigns over.
Snapped from your subconsciously angry state,
And launched back into yourself again
As if time begins to slow down for moments,
While nothing is said.
There is crying, there is destruction.
You are angry but hurt.
achieved expression
But wished that you hadn't been so blunt.
A side hidden to the world, but always there.
Tell me,
Do you pick-up razor-sharp shards of glass,
Knowing
that the touch cuts you constantly
while you yell in pain
Or, do you step on and over them,
Knowing
that you're forsaking a relationship of good times?

THE PUSH

On the other hand, I sometimes feel as if anger is one of the best emotions to feel. Many people say, "you can't do anything right when you're angry". Personally, I beg to differ.

I think anger is that open door that we walk through, where things push us to do better things in life. It's as if the things you do have a certain edge, heightened sense, and true meaning behind it. Here, it's as if you feel no emotion or pain. This is where the adrenaline kicks in. In a sense, it's as if time itself begins to move faster, you feel that extra kick to get up and go.

HAPPINESS

DEAR READER:

What a blissful mood I find myself in as I write this piece crafted for you. Joyful is my mood, as I hope that this brings some sunshine into your time today reading this. If no one has told you today, you are an amazing person, filled with amazing potential.

Beginning to walk differently, speak sweetly, and glow brightly, and everything seems to be alright. The hope that was never there, begins to smother and act as a blanket that comforts and encourages you. The little things and the big things that we find throughout ourselves, as well as others. Our happiness is our best kept secret, and most powerful weapon. It keeps us alive on the inside, and youthful on the outside. Personally, finding happiness makes you feel good, and turns your outlook on life from negative to positive.

LIFTED

Happiness lifting us up
To a new high
Knocking us off
Pushing us up
On the altitude away from attitude
Radiance filled
Sweet speech
Happiness is a leech
Sentimental things matter to me
The golden joy
Pure at heart
The best kept secret is life itself

FEELING SO UP

The feeling itself on the inside made me feel alive. Think of the sunflowers in the sun, with dandelion seeds blowing in the wind. Just as the sun comes out for its daily visit, the sunflowers look even more appealing and free. I imagined myself as that sunflower. When my sun of happiness came to shine, it was as if nothing in this world could tarnish the happiness inside.

Golden rays both illuminate a path of destiny written by one beyond the moon and stars, as well as the vision seen for the future.

As my heart beats with new life and meaning, I started to explore the new and unknown with courage. Most importantly, there was nothing to bind me to the weight of the world that followed grief and sadness. I felt and looked just fine.

SMILE

Drifting to a place where you reside
With feelings so encouraging and kind

As the sun kissed my forehead warm
I rose with a spirit followed in form
How kind of a visit to my daily adventures
What happened, I promise was lately none self-centered

Following me around a block where I suddenly jumped
Not too high to give my head a thump
But, How nice and refined
Rain and storms seem to line
The silver and gold in my life
The cleansed me of revenge and strife

How quaint to be able to paint
A canvas full of memories with no taint
Tonality and range,
With the deepest depth, and accurate aim
You came to visit me
Ever so calmy
Giving me a smile, and sweetly
Guiding me, and never leaving

Digging into myself, I walked differently, and people swore I had changed, but I like to think that I refined around the edges. Think of how gardeners cut and trim around the hedges, I like to think of this as the making up and decoration of my image and life.

SUPPORT

Whenever you feel down
Look and understand
That I'm here to take your hand
Leading you through and by
Away from your pain and struggle

I'm here for you
In the back of your mental
That tiny ray of sunshine
Because I remember when you were mine

Never truly alone
Accepting that things
will never be perfect
But smiles and chuckles are nice to have
When there's nothing to hold

At night when you're lonely
Take my hello and a parting pass
A port pass trip to the stars
For a power trip back around the sun
Down to earth, which is where you'll find me
In between the space where only time
And goldmines exist in the form of hugs
And smiles that bring you everlasting support

CONCLUSION

DEAR READER,

This chapter allowed me to utilize my anger and points of happiness and write based off the energy that came upon me. Being able to convey the feelings through rhythms, rhymes, and phrases that you may find odd, striking, or unique is the greatest satisfaction in my little world Hopefully, you discover more, and embark upon the next chapter. Until then, take some time to reflect on yourself, your feelings and traits, and most importantly yourself. Feel free to turn as many pages as needed.

WISHING YOU THE WIDEST ARRAY OF EMOTIONS IN ALL THE WORLD,

AYLAH.BIRKS.

SADNESS AND FEAR

DEAR READER:
Sometimes it can be loud, roaring away at you. It can tear at your soul and spirit, breaking you down slowly, but effectively. Other times, it's sneaky, but deadly. You constantly find yourself looking over your shoulder of what used to be.

DESCRIPTION AND DEPICTION

It sometimes came onto me like a rogue wave,
while other times felt like something unable to be explained,
creeping onto my spirit,
and looming over me
like a dark shadow from a corner.
I was then launched onto never ending roller coaster
that had its highs and lows.
The sadness I felt
was the kind that rips at you
Batters you
And flips you from side to side.

It was the unforgettable type
that lingers on
long after the damage was done.
the kind that slows you down,
and keeps you up at night
wondering, hoping, and wishing
for it to all disband.

To this day, we all wrestle with the demons and monsters that haunted us as children. It fractures your life and makes pieces shattered to a point to where you cannot repair them. So, such things begin to create holes throughout each chapter of your life filled will anger and rage, but the overarching figure remains as sadness. The fire and poisonous ash that fills these holes gives us that bitter taste in our mouths and vocabulary. Inflaming us, and causing familial rifts, and civil wars in our minds, leaves us living

restlessly in this life of endless actions. I am coming out as one of those victims. Still, I sometimes deal with the damage of the flashbacks of restless nights full of sleep, and sunny days full of rain.

As a matter of fact, this damage left a fingerprint on my soul that will never be able to be dusted off.

A FEELING ARISING

Presenting itself in many ways, forms, and fashions,
It is an emotion so raw with passion,
That it cuts through bone.
It can be so painful to have and own,
Feeling like salt soon
Being poured into a wound.
It stings, and it burns
And causes that which is around you to turn
To seem hopeless and bare.
Like Nothing is there,
Or so it seems,
To protect you, keep you safe in between
Or comfort you, to keep you thankful.
You feel gripped by the ankles
Making your teeth grit,
As you're pulled into a pit
Of something unsafe
That seems like it cannot be escaped.

At that time, I began to put up shields and barricades around myself, so that no one in the world could enter. I felt that anyone could not understand that immense grief and depression that I went through. I often sat, crying in silence, while my insides screaming for liberation, as they were locked by this overarching feeling that someone was talking and constantly chastising.

FEAR

DEAR READER:

INTRODUCTION TO FEAR

Flight and failure
Rise and fall
Paralyzing or in motion
Fear can change it all

Jumping, going forward, and high
Soaring with wings outstretched wide
Correcting your mistakes
Thinking of the next moves to take
Feeling the moment, but for a minute you fall
Because fear can change it all

Looking at the hurdles ahead
Turning your back to them instead
Ceasing to tackle the issues in life
Your courage begins to suffice
With doubt and limitations beginning to crawl
Realizing that fear has changed it all

NO EXEMPTION

I am not exempt to fear
For me,
It always the things that aren't here
That capture my attention, causing me to see
Something others don't during the day
Hearing things in the black of night
I wonder what they might say
If I described, what was seen in my sight?
I think at some point, I hit my all-time low. It was like I wasn't living my life how I wanted to live. It felt like I was controlled by this inanimate object. The weight of the world fell on my shoulders, as well as my mind.
The low self-confidence came, and I became sensitive. At the time, I didn't know my full potential, because it had been overshadowed by fear.

PARANOIA

My senses are high
The air layered so thickly
My heart rate jumps, while my breathing is jacked up into the sky
I think I see something, so quickly
In the corner of my eye,
I snap my neck to look to my left side

I swing my arms and kick out my legs
Something feels as if it's crawling on my forehead
I clutch my chest
And hope for the best
The mind is funny
For the things it makes you do
Being afraid of the things you don't see,
Making you believe in things that are invisible and not true

The games and fright
The bits I laughed at
and watched other people go through
But when it comes out at night
Sense exits, while impossible thoughts begin to lurk and crawl

My eyes are bucked and wide
Hearing like a hound
Forming fists, with sweating palms on the inside
But I'm alert pound for pound

Jumping at the sounds of my own footsteps
Growing tired, but never could I have slept
Feeling this level of fear
As little sounds turned loud fill your ear.

I walk in the silence of darkness
But the loudness of the night
I begin swinging more of less
Because I feel something touch my shoulder,
And something brush across my chest

Turning on the lights
After putting up a fight
Within my eyes is the look of fright
But nothing is there,
While down the long hallway I stared
Of things invisible and not true
Because of the crazy things that our minds make us do.

CONCLUSION

DEAR READER,

While writing this chapter, I felt feelings that hadn't been felt in a while in order to form the crux of this chapter. Anyways, we've got a long way to go, and frankly my loves, we're just scratching the surface of the wonders and works to come. Feel free to turn the page and go wherever your mind, and emotions lead you.

WISHING ALL OF THE ALLEVIATION AND COURAGE IN THE WORLD,

AYLAH.BIRKS.

WRITING TROUBLE AND UNCERTAINTY

DEAR READER:
Nothing is more frightening that the face of an empty page. However, I also know that fright brings fuel to power many things, which is terrifying.
I was alone and secluded from the world. Words alike and foreign became for me to develop. It brought on the craziness that I never expected. It brought on emotion that could not be contained. I spiraled out of orbit, and lost track of my mind and soul. I fell to pieces with my troubles in writing and uncertainty.

ORBIT

Just like a black hole,
forward movement is brought to a standstill,
thoughts to remain trapped
in a portion of our mind,
constricting the ability
to see the light,
and for the longest time,
Why force and stress
the feeling and thoughts,
when you can write
about blank ideas
and nothing itself?

I return when you least expect it
Overjoyed, rushing to accept this
Idea that left and returned to you
And craft that was learned, which grew

CONCLUSION PT.8

DEAR READER:

Stress is highly keen and particular upon the role that it plays in certain subjects in life. Be careful with each corner you pass, because it lurks, especially in your mind. Our train tracks in memory are the ones we love in memory of, because they lost their way along its way to our lives. The thoughts forgotten and not remembered are those to the finest degree. Our mind's finest leave us each day to become angels to someone else, while their angels become our bread and butter.

Wherever your thoughts reside or travel to, I wish them safe trails and travels around and back you way.

WISHING YOUR THOUGHTS SAFE TRAVELS BACK TO YOU,

AYLAH.BIRKS.

BEING AFRICAN AMERICAN

DEAR READER:
One can never truly understand the context of depth, if they have never truly lived among the words that rode the wave of the page. In this world, hatred and bigotry the shadows and clouds that follow behind me. They have bludgeoned me and blinded me to a vision limited by acts of anger and feelings of frustration in a world supposedly full of potential.

Whoever says that words don't hurt wasn't a minority. To understand and to listen are opposites of each other. Anger and rage are just a couple of things felt living day to day in a society that sees African Americans and others on different scales.

It disturbs you deeply and taints the overview that you have on the world.

THE RAGE

RAGE

rage is a
heightened sense
to particular moments in time
it focuses
on what was stripped
taken, from an age
of innocence to prime
red is rage,
cutting you long and deep
leaving you
scarred for miles
that creates highways
bypasses stretching
like interstates,
driving on the verge
of dismemberment and memories

salty, raw
leaves your heart hollow
except for the cold spite
and nails galvanized
like the lemon sour taste
that incites and ignites
a reaction reeking
of poison arsenic
mixing gas and lightning
while gaslighting the issue
dancing around what is truly needed

the pressure building
inside of that volcano
before it erupts,
before it explodes
with anger and misconstruction
energized is the story
as it feels the need to rewrite itself
the pressure building within me
is breaking at the bone
litigation and misunderstanding
isn't everything on the table
beside the shakers
salt and pepper
what the world sees
separated and different
with taste characteristics
classified

The violence intertwined within our deep history is not only systematic, but a disgrace to a society at the head of the modern free world. For centuries, we have endured violence, violations, and humiliations. The violence has followed our name so much, many think it's an inheritance. Not only has it been witnessed, but documented on files, records, and camera.

> ### "PREJUDICE IS A BURDEN THAT CONFUSES THE PAST, THREATENS THE FUTURE, AND RENDERS THE PRESENT INACCESSIBLE."
>
> – MAYA ANGELOU

RACISM

I sit on the edge of the city that spoke to my soul, cursing it at the same time. The streetlights burst with the curbsides full. Flooded with alcohol, poured from the heartbroken families of homies broke my soul. The comments and jeers ripped at my flesh, seeing my people blow away in the winds of time that plague the day.

Ashes to ashes and dust to dust they say.

Wanting them to be here for a good time and a lifetime, not a wrong time and a short time, I figured that I had to move on.

The cracks in the lines of the sidewalk represent the cracked smile that I wear convince those that we are alright. Cracks in life's daily face is worn upon the mask of weariness, following stretchmarks of misconception and grief.

TALES FROM THE SOUTH

an African American female
caught up in the tale
from whatever the bleeding south entails
being a jack of all trades
knowing more than the expectation laid

trying to keep my mental building
inside away from the pressure building
inside
crashing on me, the rogue wave tide
hardships and advantages go hand in hand
starships and trips outlandish
all remain contraband
the back wood foreword
keeps the neighborhood from moving forward

with a gray are
we're the middle confusion
a battle for fission vs. Fusion
nuclear to be all clear,
but unclear is the motive
for the evident action
towards a child, closest

blankets quilted to suppress
the oppress, have me pressed
and laid out in obsession
to run my mouth, as my mind walks
running and walking towards the format
along the lines, violence
residing at my doormat

some of the most offensive language
expensive,
of energy and time,
make you feel powerful and extensive
utilizing and underlying
words no longer than your thumb and nail
trying to intimidate the mere minority
finding itself in me,
the new generation African American
the black butterfly, finally free

THE QUESTION

what's the worth
Of my black life on earth?
Does the world stop to realize?
Our child was left behind?
While others moved around and over,
In value and positions relentless,
Will my name become a headline?
Will I die a martyr?
Will I ever just be a black girl again?
Will I ever find my joy?
Did the world ever think,
how it would benefit me in return?
because be honest,
did you ever truly feel for me and them?
As we did for you
While the world so effortlessly called
because it needed to borrow their strength too?

SCARY DAYS

THE DAYS OF A FUTURE'S PAST ARE UPON US. I SIT IN THE BACK SEAT OF THE CAR WATCHING THE PEOPLE THAT WALK BY. I WONDE IF I'LL BE THE WITNESS TO SOMETHING THAT CAN BE SEEN IN PLAIN DAYLIGHT.

AS I WAS

I'm driving down the road
Hoping that I make it home
The anxiety of seeing flashing blue
Something not understood to you
Even if I do comply
You can't deny
I don't want to die
So, I just sat to myself and sighed
I just want to get to my destination
Not to have my obituary read by the nation
As I walk,
Outside to my neighborhood,
I walk to get mail out of a box.
I see a car stop, not like it should.
The widow rolls down with a phone in hand.
Believe it or not, I waived nicely and
They yell at me for stealing mail from a box.
A thought outside of the box.

I just want to get back to my destination,
Not to have my obituary read by the nation.

A police is called, but you don't even know my name.
A name that is on the box, but you don't believe my claim.
You are threatened and scared.
But, you're in a car yelling like your hearing's impaired.
I stand in silence.
You report the disturbance,
To the police and 12.
All because you thought I stole mail

So, I just stood and sighed,
Because I don't want to die.
I just want to get back to my destination,
Not to have my obituary read by the nation.
Because I'm just an African American girl
Trying to find her way in this world
Pleading to be left as I was

I digress back to what ifs and what nots on the things that happen in the darkness of the jungle. Hidden and undiscovered is that which has no way of preparation for the fright and fight of falling into the pit where one is made a martyr or another ticking mark in the etch of the times of the violent past unaccounted for.

THE HORROR

I am the stag of the woods
the one white conservatives chase
on every weekend
the one that narrowly escapes

I wear the blood of my brothers
on my flank and coat
As I remember the mutter and cry
Of the last words they spoke

when you're game
the game never ends
being hunted by men until the end
of my days
I doubt they'll ever make amends

over the life
and legacy to be idolized
by the speed of a bullet to the chest
chasing after the next claim to fame

I continue to run
never stopping

more shots are fired
the booms and bangs
escalate my fear to a new high

like the rising sun
I feel the heat of the slug
brush pass my skin
Two attempts, beyond reasonable doubt
they aim for me
the game is me

I cry out, like the bird
caged without logic
feeling trapped, flying not
because my wings are broken
while dreams of being black
are treated as a token
American streets,
where nothing is done

I remain being chased
sought after
pursued and stalked
with palms white as chalk
like cat to mouse
predator and prey
and just think
it repeats the cycle each day

THE DARK JUNGLE

imagination is painful
striking like the bullet of fate
that penetrates
our dreams, ripping buildings apart
builds that fear inside the heart
into the building
that I build in
holding mental capacity
while many sit and laugh at me
talking about experience gone mad
turning us into creatures
with nothing to add

constitutions and emancipations
give me paper cuts, the transformation
when my mind is the bandage
which is broken, sustaining damage
from the cover up injuries
roadblocks put there to hinder me
trying to piece me together
the wights and balances that tethered
the birds of feathers to weigh me down
in the water pulling me underground
below the canopy
into the quicksand to handle me
smother the vision, that I had of the world above
welcome to the dark jungle
where the conquistadors dug

Indeed, a frightening world awaits on our doorstep, and stays within proximity of our very footsteps as we walk through this land. As it creeps closer to the very lifestyle that we try to uphold, we try to brace ourselves for the impact. However, nothing can prepare you for the haunting and gripping emotions and announcements that are seen and heard daily.

CONCLUSION

DEAR READER:

I hope that you got as much insight out of it as I did. Throughout the evil and madness that is contained and allocated worldwide, we must continue to fight. We must not turn a blind eye to the wrongdoings, as if it's normal policy. We must not become silent, and let slurs and phrases bypass, without setting the record straight.

Although this was a tough subject to discuss, I feel as if that's more of a reason to get talking. I hope that this chapter starts the conversation, movement, and stirs feelings to continue to speak on the issues that plague our communities and social lives. I hope that you become more of an advocate throughout society, in order to make it a better place than it was before.

WISHING YOU ALL IN THE WORLD,

AYLAH.BIRKS.

BEING AFRICAN AMERICAN PT.2

DEAR READER:
I think that one of the joys in my life is being African American. Initially, I am proud to know who I am. Being able to see the world in its imperfection and truth is a blessing and curse. Knowing and understanding the underlying cause, truth, and reason are just a few things that are obvious. However, proving stereotypes wrong and beating statistics set are my day job.

I am not a number, nor can I be bought. Not only am I a woman, but I am an African American woman, and my worth is priceless.

BEING AFRICAN AMERICAN

I know who I am
A brownskin girl
With wild hair
Sometimes tame
My complexion is mildly fair
While my eyebrows are full
With legs long

My language is cool
Like early December skies
With a warm heart
Like the night
Of a hot summer's July

Determined and satisfied
My work is harder than most
Even if understanding comes easy
Relaxed in a way, because
My knowledge spans decades,
And centuries back

Although I can be angry
Maybe outraged
I am confident in my skin
And I know
That I feel accepted within

THROUGH AND THROUGH

Through my eyes
I don't see our men
As the rabid animals
That continuously hunt and eat

Thorough my ears
I try to deafen the sound
Of echoed stereotypes
Repeated and implied daily

Through my mind
I try hard not to remember
The traumatic experiences
That gave birth to waste
And complicated lifelines
Tangled in vines
That became more twisted
As the system grew more deadly roots

Through my hands
I refrain
From showing the cuts and burns
The callused portions
That were made from years of struggle
Climbing up mountains of achievement
And reaching altitudes
Of literal breathtaking heights

Through my life
I sometimes feel as if
I am the personification
Of the living struggle each day
Opening my eyes to issues
That seem awfully heavy
For my shoulders

Through my footsteps
I press my feet upon foundations
Of arguments and powder kegs
That burn me from sole to soul

But living through this all
Caused the anger that threw
Me into the mindset and dreams
Of a reality that can be more positive tomorrow

HAIR DEMANDS

Shrinkage, straightening
Crinkled hair image and some detangling
African American woman am I,
Black to soul, history I personify

Goddess of cocoa butter, tamer of humidity,
My hair is the most sacred part of me
Connects me to my past, my future, my present
reminds me as a Black woman
to never relent.

Edge control, and straightening combs
Picking through my new growth, to see how it's grown
African American woman, here I go
Supporting myself, even if someone is a no show

Products and toiling
hot outside and boiling
But the hair that holds and becomes my wings
Sends me to fly heights into my nearest dreams

AFRICAN AMERICAN WOMAN

African American woman
You are beautiful,
And full of potential
There is so much more to you,
Than your hips and thighs
You're just as unique as each moment,
In the fabric of time

THE MAN OF THE CULTURE
A friend told me being an African American male made him feel misrepresented, disrespected, and mutilated. Having to deal with the weight of issues that lie on the shoulders of minority men far and wide is indeed taxing. However, I think that it's time to make some important acknowledgements to those who work tirelessly around the clock for not only themselves, but for the ones surrounding them. The effort going into getting that special haircut, tying the tie just right, or specially hand picking an outfit to make an impression on the general public.
I have decided to dedicate these poems to him, and to the other men out there who need some encouragement.

THE IDEAL MAN

Enough about the anger
and spiteful actions
that can make a man go bizarre.
Here are the things
making men more special
than what they are.

An African American male
who walks with his head up high,
Shoulders not slouched,
with hands down by his side
And he speaks loud and articulate,
It draws you
toward his direction in specific.
Not only that,
but he carries himself clean and neat.
He wakes up early,
because he gets good sleep
While attacking the day
with a jump and a leap
He maintains his style and dynamic,
a real commodity.
Giving reverence to those
providing for their families
They obtain degrees,
and assist the community,
And even come home each day
to see and share the day with their families.
He's a hard worker,
thinking with his head

working with his hands
Knowing his worth,
can't be bought nor read
Because his time is expensive
And his name is his brand

As a male period, there is a sense of pride that should be naturally instilled within you. However, when that pride is being diminished time after time again, the resentment and anger sets in. It's understandable to be angry at the public that claim to support something and bend the rules behind the statement. It is disrespectful, and demeaning, but it gives you a greater chance and inspiration to achieve better for yourself, and the others around you. Understand that the road was not as easy for them to obtain the confidence, with the many wretched things that could have been thrown at him. There is nothing more to do than to respect him. Not only for his attitude, or personality, but for holding his head up in a society that doesn't often give him the props that he deserves.

TO MY AFRICAN AMERICAN MEN

To my African American men
Despite that we have different mothers
I stand by you
And encourage you to do
Better than what has already been done
So that you set the tone for your daughter and son

To my darker skinned friends
I appreciate you,
From the depths within
You are so strong in stride
And your potential and power stretches so wide
I value the way you move,
Not only in chess
But through life,
Not to mention the way you've found your groove
Cause you've been looking your best

To my brown, and tanned man
Understand,
How important you are
Know that the richest prizes
Are chased constantly,
Near and far
Understand how you are beautifully designed
And that you're not just one standing in line

To my wavy, and faded guy
I see how hard you try
To make dreams concrete

And stay away from the streets
You are intelligent and determined
And whatever you do,
You must keep going

To my activist,
Always be my optimist
Although I can't feel your pain
Of seeing the society stay the same
Of hearing the family being strained
Having a nightmare, being locked down in chains
Know that my feelings towards you will never change
Dust these issues and regain
The presence that you used to claim
Remember you are a king
A bright firework worth the sparking

To my African American brother
calm your adrenaline
As tensions are rising
While the gunshots and teargas start flying
Keep us from wearing grief and black
And take your rightful place back.

THERE IS HOPE

HOPE IS ONE OF THE GREAATEST SIDEKICK IN THIS HISTORY OF LIFE. ALTHOUGH THE INCOMES AND THROUGH-COMES OF LIFE CAN GET A BIT FRISKY AND FRUSTRATING, HOPE IS THERE TO PICK US UP, LETTING US KNOW THAT EVERYTHING CAN AND WILL BE ALRIGHT.

THE PROMISE FORM A BETTER TOMORROW MUST BE FILLED WITH FAITH, AND LACED AROUND THE TONGUE, BUT IT'S TRUE VIRTUE LIES IN HOPE. UNDERSTANDING THAT EDUCATION AND COMMUNICATION OUR ROUTES TO BRIGHTER HORIZONS WHERE ADVERSITY FORMERLY RESIDES SHOULD BE RECOGNIZED ON A PLAYING FIELD, WHETHER IT MAY BE LEVEL OR SHORT SIDED.

FOR US AND OTHERS, HOPE IS A STEP AWAY FROM THE HURT AND CURSES THAT WE HAVE FACED. HOLDING ON TO ALL OF THE ANGER AND WRONGDOING IS INDEED TIRING, AS IT RUNS THROUGH THE RACETRACK OF OUR MIND. THE NOISE A BURNING TIRES, BLOWOUTS, AND ENDLESS POTHOLES HOLD US BACK FROM HAVING THE HOPE THAT THE ROAD WILL BE SMOOTHER IN THE FUTURE FOR US.

WE CAN NEVER FORGET THE STRENGTH AND THE HOPE THAT WAS GIVEN TO US, MEANT FOR US TO RISE AND BREAK DOWN PEDESTALS.

JOURNEY TO THE PAST

I always wanted to venture back into the past
See what life was like
When they built pyramids from the bottom up
Just like life
Note the we are pyramids with strong foundations
With tunnels and secrets that lead to new destinations
A roadmap of stops and stories with each scar
Telling of adventures, picture it
Us as explorers seeing new heights
We soar high to reach mountaintops
Through the sights of the eye
Which is the verdict and jury one in all
Innocent, captivating, capturing
Landmarks in seconds like cameras
Flashing and snapping like seconds on clocks
Letting us know that it's time to come back
To the edge of the Earth through pyramids and salt rocks
Where we first took off on our story

SOCIETAL SUNRISE

As the darkness began to roll away,
Differing in direction, farther than a soft wind could convey
Thundering clouds began to part
But not too tough, to cause a whirlwind to start

I climbed to the treetops, in a hurried fashion
Pushing my way through branches and crooks, in order to fasten
Not worrying if I scratched my hands, and brought ash to my knees
Raging with the excitement, and fear that my eyes would soon see

Sore palms and tired arms
I struggled during that last bit, which caused no harm
Wondering how much more could I bare to hold on
Found myself screaming in frustration, feeling that I could not go on

Reaching the top was no easy stretch
What a sight to fetch
I found it quite rewarding finding hives of honey guarded by leaves
As I heard the sound of escaping bees

And there I found it, the sunrise of society new
Shining gold, over a sea colored deep blue
Unified, hands conjoined, and the new sun emerged
Singing the praises of a new nation, healed and purged

From domestic and foreign threats of a kind
With tears forming in the ducts of mine
Falling to water seeds earlier sowed in time
And growing to unify the wounds
of a land whose life was on the line.

CONCLUSION

DEAR READER:

It's been a bittersweet feeling for me trying to close a topic so broad, while bringing a wonderful closing as well. Paying homage while writing about my history and culture has brought me through a whirlwind of emotions. On some days, I felt powerless, while other days left me feeling empowered and strong in who I am. Being African American and having a knowledge of where I come from has been my latest and greatest inspiration for this chapter.

WISHING YOU ALL OF THE CONFIDENCE IN THE WORLD.

AYLAH.BIRKS.

ACKNOWLEDGEMENTS

To all of those who contributed to the book, this wouldn't be possible without you all. You all kept me inspired during my darkest times, and for that and many other reasons, I remain forever grateful to you.

I love you all deeply.

Cindy Birks, Teresa Birks, Jessica Walden, R.Cornelius Spencer, Erica Walton, Cedric Curry Sr., Sallie Gary, Dorothy Adside, Peggy Curry, Christopher Glover, Jacklen McFadden, Clint Jordan, Enhance our Community Foundation, LuvBay Afrobeat Music Talk Radio, Jessie Jang, Mary Hill, Lisa McGhee, Barbara Curry, Dr. Mack Bullard, Mary E. Davis, Tamira M. Moon, Deborah Little, Mesa Miller, Chandra Wilder, Lula Curry - Williams, Shirley Person, Pamela Shinholster, Nicole Huston, Betty Jean Rouse, Alexandria Lewis, Rhonda King, Nicole Meadows, Robbie Curry Sr., Yoshika Eason, Randy J. Paschal, Catherine Stolarski, Cedric Davis, Lekara Simmons, Angela Curry, Craig Curry, Rev. Dr. Willie Batts Jr., Makarios Sampson, Miriam Rearden, Gwendolyn H.

Riggins, Tameika Bond, Vickie Hill, Kate Hewitt, Terence Pennyman, Alexis Neesmith, Lemuel Brown, Javandon Shropshire, Velva Hicks, Alex Cooper, Faith Wigfall, Orena Floyd, Shalah Scott, Ernest Stackhouse, Constance Long, Allison North, Tina Thames, Joel Dukes, Dr. Linda Ramsey, The M.A. Evans Academy, Twiggs County Public School Systems, Mercer University, and the endless amount of family and friends that have loved and supported me throughout the years.

And to my entire team of editors, cover designers, and authors coaches, I thank you for always advocating for me, standing by my side, and keeping me in line during this process. You all kept me inspired during my darkest times, and for that and many other reasons, I remain forever grateful to you.

www.ingramcontent.com/pod-product-compliance
Lightning Source LLC
LaVergne TN
LVHW011840060526
838200LV00054B/4115